Fractured Fairy Tales

Grades 2-4

Written by Marie-Helen Goyetche
Illustrated by Tom Goldsmith

About the author: Marie-Helen Goyetche is an elementary school teacher and a freelance writer. She has published over 100 articles and 30 curriculum books. She lives with her husband and two sons.

ISBN 978-1-55035-861-2
Copyright 2007
Revised July 2007
All Rights Reserved * Printed in Canada

Published in the United States by:
On The Mark Press
3909 Witmer Road PMB 175
Niagara Falls, New York
14305
www.onthemarkpress.com

Published in Canada by:
S&S Learning Materials
15 Dairy Avenue
Napanee, Ontario
K7R 1M4
www.sslearning.com

At a Glance

Learning Expectations / Literacy Skills	Choral Speaking	The Stinky Cheeseman	Friends	Huge Blue Sweatshirt	Jack and the Beanstalks	Joey the Great	Prince Artee's Hobby	Simon and the Three Cats	The Elves and the Messmaker	The Right-One Prince	The Three Little Raccoons	Cinderfella	Extension Activities	Writing Fractured Fairy Tales
• Identify and describe story elements	•		•	•	•	•	•	•	•	•	•	•	•	•
• Summarize/recall events and details	•		•	•	•	•	•	•	•	•	•	•	•	•
• Character traits, comparisons	•		•	•	•	•	•	•	•	•	•	•		•
• Use context clues (e.g., identify analogies)		•			•					•				
• Make inferences (e.g., why events occurred, characters' thoughts and feelings, etc.)	•		•	•		•	•	•	•	•	•			
• Activate prior knowledge	•	•			•			•		•	•	•		•
• Understand abstract concepts – such as feelings, exaggeration, conflict, etc.				•	•				•		•			
• Evaluate information			•	•				•	•	•	•		•	
• Visualize			•	•		•	•		•	•	•	•	•	
• Question	•		•										•	•
• Predict events		•	•	•	•	•	•	•	•	•	•			
• Word meanings – word play								•	•	•	•		•	•
• Sequence events and details	•	•	•											
• Use grammar		•	•	•	•	•			•		•	•		
• Exercise creative skills	•	•	•		•	•	•	•	•	•	•		•	•

Fractured Fairy Tales

Table of Contents

Teacher Rubric Evaluation: Writing Tasks

Name of Student: _____   Title: _____

	1	2	3	4
Begining Middle End	The sentences are not in any order	There is some attempt at Beginning/Middle/End	Beginning/Middle/End are all present	Interesting and complete Beginning/Middle/End
Ideas	The main idea is not clear	The idea needs to be worked on	There is one main idea	There is one main idea and sub idea(s)
Details	Details need to be added	More details are needed	You have many details	You have many excellent details
Vocabulary	The same words are used over and over again	You used one to two new word(s)	You used many new words and expressions	Excellent vocabulary
Clearness	The piece does not make sense	The piece is somewhat clear	The piece is clear	The piece is clear, and the audience is targeted
Creativity	No creativity is shown in the piece	Try to be more creative	Some creativity and originality	Very creative and original

Student Self-Evaluation Rubric: Writing Tasks

Name of Student: _____   Title: _____

	1	2	3	4
Begining Middle End	My sentences are not in any order	I made an attempt to include a Beginning/Middle/End	I wrote a clear Beginning/Middle/End	Interesting and complete Beginning/Middle/End
Ideas	What is my main idea?	My idea needs to be worked on	I have one main idea	I have one main idea and sub idea(s)
Details	I don't have any details	I need to add more details	I have written many details	I show many excellent details
Vocabulary	I use the same words over again	I used one to two new word(s)	I have used many new words	I used difficult and well-chosen vocabulary
Clearness	My work does not make sense	My work is somewhat clear	My work is clear	My work is clear, and I know who my audience is
Creativity	I don't try to show creativity	I should try to be more creative	I show some creativity and originality	I show creativity and originality

Teacher or Peer Writing Checklist

Title: _____   Written by: _____

1	There is a good sentence for the beginning paragraph.	
2	There are sentences for the body of the piece.	
3	There is a good sentence in the concluding paragraph.	
4	The idea is present and clear.	
5	There are details that make the piece interesting.	
6	The message is clear.	
7	The sentences are clear and well written in paragraphs.	
8	There are new and difficult words.	
9	There is not any repetition.	
10	Capitals, periods, and punctuation have been checked.	
11	The good copy is ready to be written.	

Comments:_____

Recommendations by:_____

Student Writing Checklist

Title: _____   Written by: _____

1	I have a good sentence for the beginning paragraph.	
2	I have sentences for the body of the piece.	
3	I have a good sentence in my concluding paragraph.	
4	I have an idea and it is clear.	
5	I added details to make it interesting.	
6	My message is clear.	
7	My sentences are clear and well written in paragraphs.	
8	I chose my words carefully.	
9	I did not repeat the same ideas or words.	
10	I have checked it for capitals, periods, and punctuation.	
11	I am ready to now start my good copy.	
12	I am proud of and happy with my work.	

Fractured Fairy Tales

Introduction

Children adore fractured fairy tales. By utilizing their interest you can use this book to guide children to master, create, and reflect. This book is designed to encourage students to play with words, rethink the differences, and elaborate the stories they enjoy.

Fractured Fairy Tales has been organized into sections on choral speaking, the novel *The Stinky Cheese Man and Other Fairly Stupid Tales*, original fractured fairy tales plus extension activities, and writing your own fractured fairy tales.

Evaluation:

For any of the writing activities you can use the Teacher Rubric. There is a self-evaluation version of the rubric as well which can be used by children to see how they will be evaluated and what aspects are important.

When we write stories, we have many things to consider: capitals, periods, sentence structure, verbs, words, clarity. The student can use the Writing Checklist as a memory tool to remember how to write and make their writing the best possible. The teacher can use the Writing Checklist as a pre-evaluation tool before marking, and it is also suitable for peer evaluation.

Resources:

You will find six generic graphic organizers included that can be used with all the stories in the book. For example, you can have students compare the fractured tales with the original fairy tales.

Also included in this book is a listing of popular fractured fairy tales available from various publishers. Any of these can be added to a fractured fairy tale theme, while still making use of the generic activities within this book.

To inspire curiosity, there is a Fractured Fairy Tales Word Search included which uses 18 names found in the various stories.

Choral Speaking Fractured Fairy Tales:

Two choral speaking fractured fairy tales are included, where the children become an interactive part of the story. The children are given out parts, and every time their part is mentioned they follow in cue with the saying or sound. They must listen carefully to respond in the appropriate way and at the appropriate time. Instructions on how they can write their own choral speaking story is provided, along with a worksheet where they can write their own story step-by-step. This activity can be done on any theme and can be done in pairs or in small groups.

Fractured Fairy Tale Novel Study:

A novel study is included based on the popular stories written by Jon Scieszka and Lane Smith, *The Stinky Cheese Man and Other Fairly Stupid Tales*. Scrambled words, sequencing and riddles will help in both language arts skills and thought processing.

Fractured Fairy Tales

Original Fractured Fairy Tales:

Ten fractured fairy tales are included, each accompanied by discussion questions based on Bloom's Taxonomy. These questions have been developed to address six levels of competencies: **1.** knowledge; **2.** comprehension; **3.** application; **4.** analysis; **5.** synthesis; **6.** evaluation. As the level gets higher the questions get more complex and therefore the answers will get more difficult and thoughtful.

Extension Activities:

The extension activities can be used with any of the original fractured fairy tales. Worksheets to guide students in the writing of their own fractured fairy tales are also included.

A short answer key is provided at the end of the book. Enjoy *Fractured Fairy Tales*!

How to use Graphic Organizers

Venn Diagram: Children retain more information when they have a chance to compare the information with something or someone relevant in their lives. Have the students compare themselves with one of the characters in the story, or have them compare a character from a fractured fairy tale with the original. Venn diagrams can also be used to compare stories, details, and other comparable information.

You Are the Sunshine of My Life: Building webs are an important aspect of creating a story. The analogy of using the sun is clear to young children. The more rays the sun has, the brighter the sun will shine. Therefore, the more branches you fill from the sun to help you build your story the more details you will get. This will result in a better story.

Fact or Fiction: Children of this age group are often confused as to what is real and what is fiction. Many take suggestions literally as if it was the truth, especially if they see it in print. Have fun with your student dissecting the stories to see what is fact and what is fiction. Some stories will have more of one than the other. The important point is for the students to be able to recognize the differences or to question themselves.

Connections: Children need to build upon their knowledge. Fractured fairy tales are popular because the stories are already familiar to the students, making building on prior knowledge a possibility. Have the students make connections as they read the stories. There are no right or wrong answers here; making connections is the key.

Word Finder: Children need to look at the stories and see which words they need to look up, find the definition and use the word in a sentence. This word finder activity will allow the child to look up the words that she or he find difficult rather than a predetermined vocabulary list.

Sequencing: In order to be able to write stories in a logical sequence, students must be able to say and write down other stories in order. Have them practice rewriting the information down in their own words while they are picking out important passages in the story.

Venn Diagram

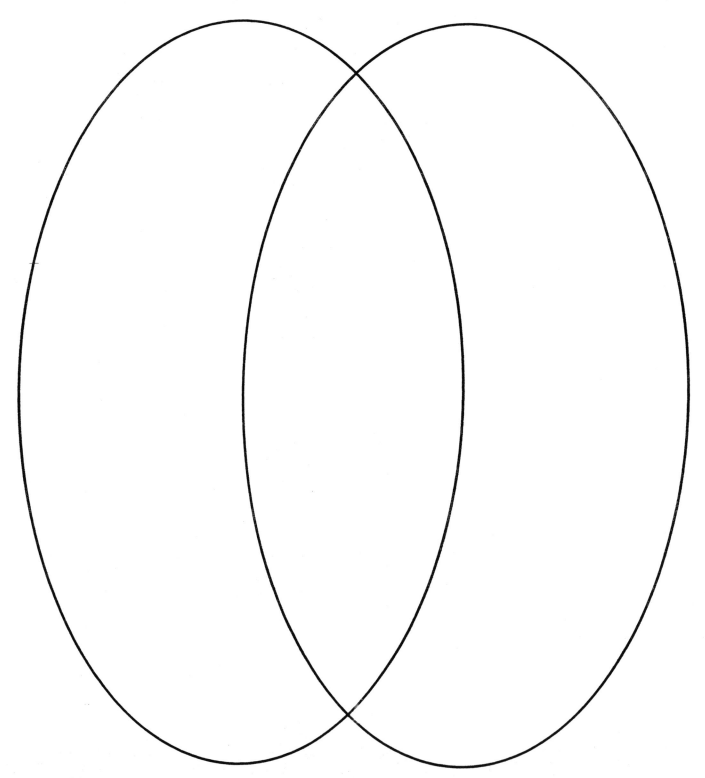

You Are the Sunshine of My Life

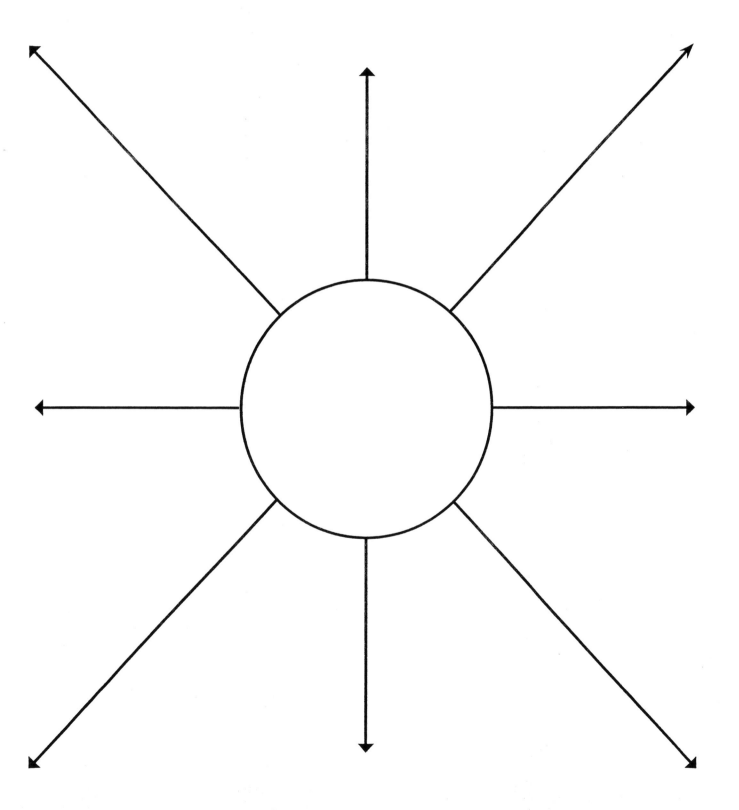

Fact or Fiction

Fact	Fiction

Connections

Passage in the story...	My connection...

Word Finder

Write new words below, with their definitions.

1. _____

2. _____

3. _____

4. _____

5. _____

6. _____

7. _____

8. _____

9. _____

Sequencing

Write the story in your own words starting with the first thing that happened.

1.	
2.	
3.	
4.	
5.	
6.	
7.	
8.	
9.	

Other Fractured Fairy Tales

Albert, Janet and Allen. *The Jolly Postman*. Boston: Little, Brown & Company, 1996. (Ages 7 up)

Albert, Janet and Allen. *The Jolly Christmas Postman*. Boston: Little, Brown & Company, 1991. (Ages 7 up)

Atwood, Margaret. *Princess Prunella and the Purple Peanut*. Toronto: Key Porter, 1995. (Ages 8 up)

Briggs, Raymond. *Jim and the Beanstalk*. New York: Coward, McCann & Geohegan, Inc., 1970. (Ages 5-7)

Buehner, Caralyn. *Fanny's Dream*. New York: Dial Books for Young Readers, 1996. (Ages 7 up)

Cole, Babette. *Prince Cinders*. Hamish Hamilton's Children's Books, 1987. (Ages 6 up)

Cole, Babette. *Princess Smartypants*. Putnam Publishing Group, 1987. (Ages 6 up)

Emberley, Michael. *Ruby*. Toronto: Little, Brown and Company, 1990. (Ages 7-9)

French, Fiona. *Snow White in New York*. Oxford: Oxford University Press, 1986. (Ages 7-8)

Jackson, Ellen B. *Cinder-Edna*. New York: Lothrop, Lee & Shepard, 1994. (Ages 5-7)

Little, Jean and Maggie de Vries. *Once upon a Golden Apple*. Toronto: Viking, 1991. (Ages 5-7)

Lowell, Susan. *The Three Little Javelinas*. Northland, 1992. (Ages 5-7)

Minters, Frances. *Cinder-Elly*. New York: Viking, 1994. (Ages 7-9)

Mossie, Diane Redfield. *Briar Rose and the Golden Eggs*. New York: Parents' Magazine Press, 1973. (Ages 5-7)

Munsch, Robert. *The Paper Bag Princess*. Toronto: Annick Press, 1982. (Ages 5 up)

Palatini, Maggie. *Piggie Pie*. New York: Clarion Books, 1995. (Ages 7 up)

Ross, Tony. *Mrs. Goat and Her Seven Little Kids*. London: Andersen Press, 1989. (Ages 6-7)

Schertle, Alice. *Bill and the Google-Eyed Goblins*. New York: Lothrop, Lee & Shepard Books, 1987. (Ages 6-9)

Scieszka, Jon. *The Frog Prince Continued*. London: Puffin Books, 1991. (Ages 7 up)

Scieszka, Jon. *The Stinky Cheese Man and Other Fairly Stupid Tales*. New York: Viking, 1992. (Ages 7 up)

Scieszka, Jon. *The True Story of the 3 Little Pigs*. New York: Viking, 1989. (Ages 7-9)

Tolhurst, Marilyn. *Somebody and the Three Blairs*. New York: Orchard Books, 1990. (Ages 5-7)

Trivizas, Eugene. *The Three Little Wolves and the Big Bad Pig*. New York: Scholastic Inc., 1994. (Ages 5-7)

Tunnell, Michael O. *Beauty and the Beastly Children*. New York: Tambourine Books, 1993. (Ages 7-9)

Turkle, Brinton. *Deep in the Forest*. New York: E.P. Dutton & Co., Inc., 1976. (Ages 4-7)

Van Woerkom, Dorothy. *The Queen Who Couldn't Bake Gingerbread*. New York: Alfred A. Knopf, 1975.

Waddell, Martin. *The Tough Princess*. New York: Philomel Books, 1986. (Ages 5-7)

Wahl, Jan. *The Prince Who Was a Fish*. New York: Simon and Schuster, 1970. (Ages 6-9)

Wegman, Cinderella. *Cinderella*. New York: Hyperion, 1993. (Ages 6-8)

Wegman, Cinderella. *Little Red Riding Hood*. New York: Hyperion, 1993. (Ages 6-8)

Williams, Jay. *Petronella*. New York: Parents' Magazine Press, 1973. (Ages 6-9)

Williams, Jay. *School for Sillies*. New York: Parents' Magazine Press, 1969.

Yeoman, John and Quentin Blake. *The Wild Washerwomen*. New York: Greenwillow Books, 1979. (Ages 6-9)

Yolen, Jane. *The Simple Prince*. New York: Parents' Magazine Press, 1978. (Ages 6-9)

Yolen, Jane. *Sleeping Ugly*. New York, Coward-McCann, Inc., 1981. (Ages 6-9)

Fractured Fairy Tale Word Search

```
V E L V E T E E N A
A S M Z S B C L K R
L W O S R M O V I T
L E Z Z Z Z O E N E
E A Z Z Z K S G E E
F T N A I C I G A M
R S H U G E E T S R
E H B L U E I K Z B
D I Z Z Y M E Z Z U
N R Z E M E Z Z Z U
I T O Y H S I M O N
C J A C K N I G H T
```

Characters found in these fractured fairy tales.

Artee	Blue	Cheeks
Cinderfella	Cookie	Elves
Huge	Jack	Joey
King	Knight	Magician
Mr. Buun	Mr. Sow	Simon
Sweatshirt	Timmy	Velveteen

The Magician

MASTER OF CEREMONIES:	"Ladies and Gentlemen"
RAOUL THE MAGICIAN:	"ABRABRACACADADABRABRA"
CROWD:	"OO wow"
CUTE LITTLE GIRL:	"I'm so cute!"
PEPPER:	A Loud Sneeze

The fair was back in town with its new fall line up. The **MASTER OF CEREMONIES** could be heard in front of the theater as he shouted, "Come one, come all – pay your admission to see many wonderful magicians. Coming up soon, the incredible **RAOUL THE MAGICIAN**. Come and seek a thrill. Discover the mysteries behind one of the world's most famous magicians." The **CROWD** quickly lined up and got their tickets. Little did they know what magic waited.

"Ladies and gentlemen," bellowed the **MASTER OF CEREMONIES**. "Let me introduce to you the most magnificent and mysterious magician in the world, **RAOUL THE MAGICIAN**." The **CROWD** cheered.

The world famous magician came in with a huge smile upon his face. He took off his top hat and twirled it in the air. "Welcome dear **CROWD**," said **RAOUL THE MAGICIAN**. "Let me amaze your eyes. For this trick, I'll need a volunteer!"

"Me, pick me," said a **CUTE LITTLE GIRL** who was no more than four or five years old. The **CROWD** showed their approval.

"All right, then, I shall pick you, **CUTE LITTLE GIRL**. Come up. For this trick I'll also need some water in a see-through glass and some **PEPPER**." **RAOUL THE MAGICIAN** continued. "Now I shall sprinkle a lot of **PEPPER** in the glass of water. Now, **CUTE LITTLE GIRL**, can you put a finger in the glass of water and make the **PEPPER** separate."

The **CUTE LITTLE GIRL** tried with her right index finger. However, that did not work, the **PEPPER** stayed. **CUTE LITTLE GIRL** then tried with her left index finger. Again, nothing happened, the **PEPPER** stayed in the same place.

"I will show you what to do!" exclaimed **RAOUL THE MAGICIAN**. He walked closer to the table and he put his finger in the water. Magically, the **PEPPER** separated. The **CROWD** went wild. **RAOUL THE MAGICIAN** had succeeded in separating the water and the **PEPPER**.

"What's your trick?" asked **CUTE LITTLE GIRL**. Before he could answer, **RAOUL THE MAGICIAN'S** right shoelace came untied and with his left foot, he stepped on it. As he turned toward **CUTE LITTLE GIRL**, he tripped and fell flat on his face. The **CROWD** yelled in horror. As **RAOUL THE MAGICIAN** fell, he brought the tablecloth with him, revealing the liquid soap under the table.

RAOUL THE MAGICIAN was a fraud and anyone who put liquid soap on his or her finger would have made the **PEPPER** separate.

The **MASTER OF CEREMONIES** was quick to add, "Thank you **CROWD** for your time and attention."

THE END

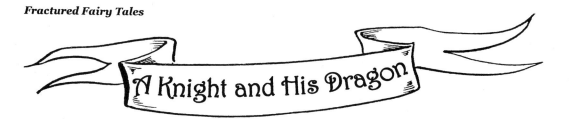

A Knight and His Dragon

KNIGHT: clank clank clank
DRAGON: ROOOOAAAR
KING: Long live the King
QUEEN: Would anyone like some tea?
PRINCESS: Help! Help! Help!
RAT: Food? Did anyone say food?

Once upon a time, in a land far, far away, there was a **KNIGHT** and his **DRAGON** who lived in a kingdom.

They both worked very hard to protect the **KING**, the **QUEEN**, and their lovely **PRINCESS**. No one in the kingdom would dare do or say anything that would upset them for they feared what the **KNIGHT** and his **DRAGON** would do in their defense. They might be thrown in with the **RATS**.

One day, the **KNIGHT** and his **DRAGON** were doing their regular training exercises when they heard a huge noise. They went to investigate throughout the castle. All they could hear, from far away, was the **PRINCESS**.

By the time the **KNIGHT** and his **DRAGON** realized something was wrong, the **PRINCESS** could not be heard anymore. The **KING** and the **QUEEN** were very concerned.

For minutes and minutes, hours and hours, the **KNIGHT** and his **DRAGON** searched the kingdom grounds for the lovely **PRINCESS** but she was nowhere to be found. That night, while they both stood out in the moonlight, Jack the **RAT** snuck up close to them and whispered, "Hey! Are you looking for the **PRINCESS**?"

"Yes!" said the **KNIGHT**. "Do you know where she is?" Jack the **RAT** did not answer.

"Come on **RAT**. Tell me where the **PRINCESS** is!" The **RAT** went on talking about the terrible living conditions he and his family and friends were enduring. Dark and musty dungeons. No windows, no light, no air. The kingdom had a shortage of prisoners and now the **RATS** had a shortage of food.

"If we sign an agreement for a regular supply of food for the **RATS** and lights to be installed in the dungeon, will you lead us to the **PRINCESS**?" asked the **KNIGHT**.

"Only if you get someone to clean the dungeon too," replied the **RAT**. The **KNIGHT** nodded in agreement. The **RAT** knew the **KING** and the **QUEEN** would agree to anything to have their **PRINCESS** back.

Jack the **RAT** went back into the castle followed by the **KNIGHT** and the **DRAGON**. He led them down to the servants' quarters where the **PRINCESS** was hiding and waiting.

"Did it work, Jack?" asked the **PRINCESS**. "Yes it did!" He hi-fived the **PRINCESS**.

From that night on, the **RAT**, the **PRINCESS**, the **KING**, the **QUEEN**, the **KNIGHT**, and the **DRAGON** all lived together in harmony in the castle. In a very clean castle!

How to Write Your Own Choral Speaking Story

Writing a choral speaking story is not difficult. It can be a lot of fun, especially if you are working in pairs or groups of three.

1. Choose a theme: medieval, fairy tale, sports, an event, etc. This could also be used for your title. For example:

   Title: "A Knight and His Dragon"

2. Choose what style: funny, sad, suspenseful, or mysterious.

3. Choose two or three characters and two or three objects that make noise. You could decide to choose five characters or five objects and that is fine. More than five is too many.

   Write the characters and their noises down. For example:

KNIGHT:	clank clank clank
DRAGON:	ROOOOAAAR
KING:	Long live the King
QUEEN:	Would anyone like some tea?
PRINCESS:	Help! Help! Help!
RAT:	Food? Did anyone say food?

4. Start writing your story. Be aware of the characters and objects you have chosen and make sure you incorporate them into your story.

Choral Speaking Worksheet

Theme?	
Style?	

Characters **OR** Objects?	Sounds?

Now you are ready to write your story.

Title: _____

_____

_____

_____

_____

_____

_____

_____

Read your story more than once to make sure it sounds right.
Practice with the people who will be sounding out the parts!

The Stinky Cheese Man and Other Fairly Stupid Tales

"The Stinky Cheese Man and other Fairly Stupid Tales" by Jon Scieszka and Lane Smith is different than other picture books. Are you a good observer? Can you find nine differences? There are at least 15 possible answers.

1. _____
2. _____
3. _____
4. _____
5. _____
6. _____
7. _____
8. _____
9. _____

The illustrations are a combination of paintings and collage. Look at the picture opposite the "Giant Story". There are 11 references to other fairy tales. How many references can you find in the collage?

1. _____   2. _____
3. _____   4. _____
5. _____   6. _____
7. _____   8. _____
9. _____   10. _____
11. _____

Cinderumpelstiltskin

This story was divided into 10 pieces, but the pieces are not in order. Can you place them in the right order?

Part of the Story	Order
"Come on. Do you think it's 'Chester'?"	
"I can help you spin straw into gold," said the little man.	
"Oh, just guess a name, any name."	
The prince announced that he was holding a fabulous ball at the castle.	
Cinderella cleaned the house, so she did not have time to get ready.	
Cinderella lived with her wicked stepmother and two ugly stepsisters.	
They changed her name to Cinderumpelstiltskin.	
The stepmother and stepsisters got all dressed up to go.	
Then she closed the door and left the little man standing outside screaming.	
"Would you like to try to guess my name?" said the clever little man.	

If you could recommend three pieces of clothing to Cinderella, what would they be?

1. _____   2. _____

3. _____

On another piece of paper, draw Cinderella's new fashion.

The Stinky Cheese Man

Can you unscramble the letters below to form words found in the story.

1. n y k t i s   ___ ___ ___ ___ ___ ___
2. e h e c e s   ___ ___ ___ ___ ___ ___
3. c a c t o s h e h m a   ___ ___ ___ ___ ___ ___ ___ ___ ___ ___
4. d g a e g g   ___ ___ ___ ___ ___ ___
5. d e z e n e s   ___ ___ ___ ___ ___ ___
6. e c a h e t r   ___ ___ ___ ___ ___ ___
7. e r d i g b   ___ ___ ___ ___ ___ ___
8. g o c u d e h   ___ ___ ___ ___ ___ ___ ___
9. w f a l u   ___ ___ ___ ___ ___
10. r e b i l e r t   ___ ___ ___ ___ ___ ___ ___

If you could make your own character out of food, what three ingredients would you use? List them below and draw your new character.

1. _____   2. _____   3. _____

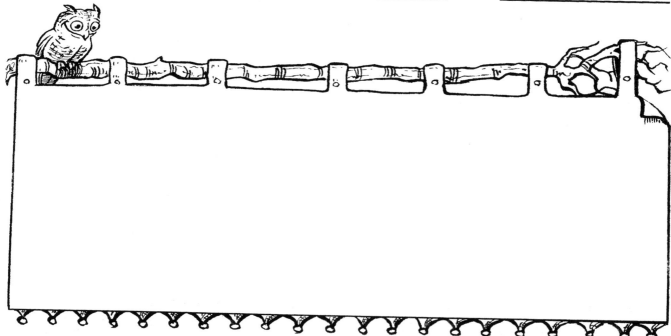

The Stinky Cheese Man and Other Fairly Stupid Tales

Can you guess the following riddles?

1. I am clever.
   I do not like smelly things.
   I can swim.
   Who am I?

   _____

2. I am tiny.
   I eat Locustidae.
   I have slimy skin.
   Who am I?

   _____

3. I am fast.
   I have two black eyes.
   I have a pork mouth.
   Who am I?

   _____

4. I am the baby.
   I have six siblings.
   I'm not a pretty swan.
   Who am I?

   _____

5. I use bone meal
   to make my bread.
   I talk in uppercase letters.
   I grabbed Jack and dragged
   him to the next page.
   Who am I?

   _____

6. I planted the wheat.
   I watered the wheat.
   I harvested the wheat.
   Who am I?

   _____

Now it is time for you to write a riddle.

7. I am_____

   I eat _____

   I love_____

   Who am I?

   _____

Can your friends guess who you wrote about?

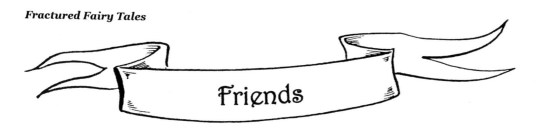

Friends

Miss Grasshopper and Mr. Ladybug are the best of friends. But for a long time, they ignored each other rather than accepting each other for who they are.

One morning, Mr. Ant was carrying a great big leaf he had taken from underneath the rubber tree plant.

"Where are you off to, Mr. Ant? Isn't your house that way?" Miss Grasshopper said, as she pointed in the other direction.

"Yes, but haven't you heard about the big storm? The birds have warned us to get to higher ground," Mr. Ant said, as he quickly walked past. "I'm going for cover at the tree trunk," he yelled.

"Thanks for the warning," yelled Miss Grasshopper. "I'll do the same thing."

Mr. Ladybug went by but Miss Grasshopper ignored him, as usual.

By the end of the day, it had started to rain. You could see and hear wiggling leaves in the wind. It was quite a storm, heavy rain, strong winds, loud thunder and very bright lightning. All the animals and the insects were hiding to protect themselves.

All except Mr. Ladybug. He was stuck on his back on the ground with a leaf on top of him. The wind was blowing very hard and he was hanging on with all his might.

Mr. Ant and Miss Grasshopper were safe and dry when Mr. Ant pointed and said, "LOOK! Mr. Ladybug is in trouble".

Miss Grasshopper looked outside.

"Get some dry leaves and some hot cocoa ready," she said as she hopped into the rain. "I'll be back," she screamed on her way out. She hopped and hopped. She was having a difficult time against the wind. She had trouble landing beside Mr. Ladybug.

"Hang on to me," she yelled. Mr. Ladybug was so tired from hanging onto the leaf that he did not refuse her invitation and jumped onto her back right away. They hopped together to safety where Mr. Ant was waiting with hot cocoa and leaves cut up in sections.

"That was pretty close," said Mr. Ant.

"Yeah, I didn't think the storm would be so bad. Miss Grasshopper, how can I ever repay you for what you have just done. I'm very grateful," said Mr. Ladybug. "Thank you."

"I'm very sorry for not warning you about the storm. I should have said something to you earlier. I'm glad you are okay now," she said.

"Me, too!" added Mr. Ladybug.

They shook legs and have been the best of friends ever since.

Discussion Questions

1. Who did not like each other at the beginning of the story but became best of friends at the end? _____

2. Who was in trouble during the storm? _____

3. What did Miss Grasshopper do in the story? _____
   _____

4. What didn't Miss Grasshopper do? _____
   _____

5. Why do you think Miss Grasshopper went to get Mr. Ladybug?
   _____

6. What do you think would have happened if she had told Mr. Ladybug about the storm?
   _____
   _____

7. What would you have done if you were Miss Grasshopper?
   _____

8. What is the lesson in this story? _____
   _____

True or False

Circle **T**, if the statement is True or circle **F**, if the statement is false.

1. Miss Grasshopper and Mr. Ladybug were always friends.   T   F
2. Mr. Ant told Mr. Ladybug about the storm.   T   F
3. The birds told Mr. Ant to get to higher ground.   T   F
4. Mr. Ladybug knew about the storm.   T   F
5. After the storm, Miss Grasshopper and Mr. Ladybug   T   F
   went back to disliking each other.

Find out More

Choose an insect that sparks your interest. Using an encyclopedia, a library book, or a web site on the Internet, find six facts about the insect you have chosen.

Insect: _____

Fact 1: _____

Fact 2: _____

Fact 3: _____

Fact 4: _____

Fact 5: _____

Fact 6: _____

Diorama

Recreate a scene from the story "Friends".

Items you will need:

A cardboard box, paints and brushes, construction paper, clay, other decorative recycled objects you may have, various crayons, glue, and scissors

Directions:

- Take a cardboard box (a shoe box is a good size).
- Decorate both the inside and the outside of the box with earth tone colors.
- Use paper, cardboard, and clay to create an outdoor forest scene.
- Add as many trees, leaves and insects as you can. Recreate the story of "Friends" as a finger puppet show using your diorama.

Huge Blue Sweatshirt

Once upon a time, there was a cute little boy. His grandfather loved him. He bought him a blue sweatshirt to wear. The boy wore it all the time even though it was much too big.

One day, the boy's mother asked him to bring some lunch to his grandfather: some yummy golden corn on the cob, some red ripe tomatoes, warm bread with fresh cheese, and some hot, homemade chicken soup. The little boy left immediately.

On the road, a bird came up to him and asked him if he needed any help. Huge Blue Sweatshirt refused the offer and continued on his way. The bird kept insisting and mentioned that his corn smelled like heaven. Huge Blue Sweatshirt thought to himself. If I eat the corn, the bird will not bother me anymore. Grandpa will not miss the corn.

That is what he did. He sat and ate the golden corn. Once he was done, he set off on his way. The bird left Huge Blue Sweatshirt alone.

On the road, a raccoon came up to him and asked him if he needed any help. Huge Blue Sweatshirt refused the offer and continued on his way. The raccoon kept insisting and mentioned that the tomatoes were very ripe. Huge Blue Sweatshirt thought to himself. If I eat the tomatoes, the raccoon will not bother me anymore. Grandpa will not miss the tomatoes.

That is what he did. He sat and rapidly ate the red ripe tomatoes. Once he was done, he set off on his way. The raccoon left Huge Blue Sweatshirt alone.

On the road, a wolf came up to him and asked him if he needed any help. Huge Blue Sweatshirt refused the offer and continued on his way. The wolf kept insisting and mentioned that the bread and cheese smelled delicious. Huge Blue Sweatshirt thought to himself. If I eat the bread and cheese, the wolf will not bother me anymore. Grandpa will not miss the bread and cheese.

That is what he did. He sat and promptly ate the warm bread and fresh cheese. Once he was done, he set off on his way. The wolf left Huge Blue Sweatshirt alone.

It was getting late and he was full. At least grandpa will have the chicken soup, he thought. He continued his trip.

Coming toward him was a great big bear. The bear asked if he needed any help. Huge Blue Sweatshirt refused the offer and continued on his way. The bear kept insisting. Huge Blue Sweatshirt thought to himself. If I eat the chicken soup, the bear will not bother me any more. Grandpa will not miss the soup.

That is what he did. He sat and ate the hot, homemade chicken soup. He was stuffed like a turkey at Thanksgiving.

The bear was upset. Huge Blue Sweatshirt took his baskets and quickly ran screaming toward his grandfather's door. His grandfather heard the commotion and got his rifle ready. He set the door open, the boy ran in, and grandfather shot the bear.

They hugged. His grandfather laughed. He was glad his grandson was alive. He thanked the boy for the bear he had brought him. It would supply him with meat for the whole winter.

THE END

Discussion Questions

1. Where was Huge Blue Sweatshirt going? _____
   _____

2. What animals approached him along the way? _____
   _____

3. Was it a good idea for him to eat all the food? _____
   _____

4. What would you have done if you were the grandfather?
   _____

5. What is the lesson in this story? _____
   _____

6. How different is this tale to "Little Red Riding Hood"? _____
   _____

True or False

Circle **T**, if the statement is true or circle **F**, if the statement is false.

1. Huge Blue Sweatshirt had to bring his grandfather   T F
   a lunch.
2. The boy's real name was Huge Blue Sweatshirt.   T F
3. The boy met many animals along the way.   T F
4. Huge Blue Sweatshirt fed the animals as he went.   T F
5. The grandfather killed the bear.   T F
6. The grandmother killed the wolf in "Little Red Riding Hood". T F
7. The grandfather was grateful and happy the boy was   T F
   still alive.
8. Huge Blue Sweatshirt ate so much, he was sick.   T F

Adjectives

In the story "Huge Blue Sweatshirt", you will find many adjectives. Adjectives are used to describe nouns (people, places and/or things). Reread the story and list at least 12 adjectives you find below.

_____   _____   _____

_____   _____   _____

_____   _____   _____

_____   _____   _____

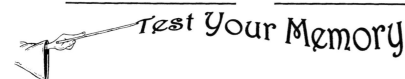

Test Your Memory

Match the animal and the food item from the story "Huge Blue Sweatshirt".

Animals: wolf   cat   raccoon   bird   bear
Food: soup   bread   cheese   corn   tomatoes

Animal	Food

Now rewrite them in the order of appearance in the story.

	Animal and Food Item
1	
2	
3	
4	

Jack and the Beanstalks

Once upon a time, there was a good student named Jack. Jack loved going to school and he did everything his teacher Mr. Sow told him to do.

One day in science class, the students planted beans. They wanted to see how long they took to grow and how many beans came from planting just one bean. Mr. Sow had extra beans left and offered them to the class. Jack's family was not wealthy. Jack thought if he could plant some beans, his family would be able to eat the beans and they would not be hungry. He brought them home.

At home, he planted beans along the east side of the house. He planted beans along the north side of the house. He planted beans along the west side of his house and then a few on the south side of the house beside the front door. Many days passed. Jack took care of watering the plants and weeding the garden and the plants grew.

They grew and grew, and soon beanstalks hid the bottom of the house. His parents were very happy. They could make bean soup, bean salad, chili, and bean dip. The beans were delicious and very nutritious.

Mr. Sow's beans were growing magically. They did not stop growing. They grew and grew, and soon the beanstalks covered the house. The family knew they were in trouble. Their house was completely surrounded by beanstalks.

"What are we going to do?" asked his father.

"We can't see through the windows because of the stalks and it is always dark," added Jack's sister.

" I don't know how to get into the house. Where's the front door?" added his younger brother.

"Where will we ever store all these beans?" asked his worried mom.

"I know exactly what to do," yelled Jack as he ran down the street.

The next morning the teachers from school showed up at Jack's house. The school buses came and delivered all the children on the front lawn. The local mall closed down for the day. The neighbors came too, and together everyone picked beans.

Some beans were sent to the canning company. Some beans were given to each of the helpers. Some beans were kept for Jack's family. The town had enough beans to feed them for years to come. And there were enough beans to give to the other towns in the area.

Jack thanked his teacher Mr. Sow for the beans. Mr. Sow told him it was nothing, and quickly added that he had just bought a big batch of strawberry seeds... He asked Jack, "Would you like some to take home?"

THE END

Discussion Questions

1. What did the teacher do in the story? _____

_____

2. Who helped Jack when it was time for harvesting? _____

_____

3. Why do you think the harvest was so productive? _____

_____

4. What do you think would have happened if the community had not helped the boy and his family? _____

_____

5. What would you have done with all those beans? _____

_____

6. What is the most important point of this story? _____

_____

7. If you could rewrite this story what role could you give to a giant?

_____

True or False

Circle **T**, if the statement is True or circle **F**, if the statement is false.

1. The family helped Mr. Sow plant the beans at school.   T F
2. The boy's house could no longer be seen.   T F
3. The family did not know what to do.   T F
4. The teachers also planted beans at their houses.   T F
5. Mr. Sow had many different kinds of beans and seeds.   T F
6. His mother was worried about storing all the beans.   T F

VERBS

In the story "Jack and the Beanstalks", you will find many verbs. Verbs are actions made in the story by the characters. Write at least 10 verbs you find in the story.

_____   _____
_____   _____

| regular |

_____   _____
_____   _____

Some of these verbs are **regular** verbs, which means we can add **_ed** to the end when we want to say the action happened in the past. Circle every verb you found that you can add _ed to the end, and draw a line to the word **regular** in the middle.

Cooking with Beans

Find a recipe in a cookbook or on the Internet that uses beans, and copy it so you can make it at home, or ask your family to make it for you.

Recipe Title:_____

Ingredients you will need:

_____   _____   _____
_____   _____   _____
_____   _____   _____

Directions:

_____
_____
_____

Joey the Great

There once was a young man named Joey. He was training to be a knight. His goal was to become knight and save the Italian Kingdom of Sardinia from the Ultimate Gildo. If Joey won, he would be named Joey the Great.

It took many years of training but Joey knew he had what it takes. He wanted to protect his kingdom. He put in hours and hours of training. People in the kingdom, on the other hand, were worried. They knew that no one had the guts or the physical strength to win against the Ultimate Gildo. They did not know Joey's plan and they feared they would lose.

During the spring, an illness swept the kingdom. Everyone was ill. People were dying and mourning. Joey was fine and healthy. He was training harder than ever. The Ultimate Gildo thought that he could easily conquer the kingdom. Now that everyone was ill it would be very simple.

The Ultimate Gildo arrived at the kingdom, secretively snooping about. He had heard that Joey was training for battle, but that everyone else was sick in bed. The Ultimate Gildo wanted to sneak up on the people and catch them off guard. He was confident he would win.

Joey had a feeling today was going to be the day of the battle and he put on all his armor. Joey told his wife that he loved her very much and that she should not worry. He asked her to always keep a special place in her heart for him. She did as he said and told him she trusted him and his strength. Joey's wife knew that the knight would win the fight against the Ultimate Gildo.

The Ultimate Gildo confronted Joey. They battled. During the early hours of the evening, the sounds of swords hitting against each other meant that both were still alive and fighting. The battle noises could be heard all over the kingdom. No one dared to move. The Ultimate Gildo was getting a little tired. He could not understand why and how Joey had so much endurance.

The battle got tougher and tougher. Both were tired and the Ultimate Gildo had to go to the washroom. The battle was very long. Many people were sleeping. The Ultimate Gildo could not take it any more, he really had to go to the washroom. Joey saw the weakness in the Ultimate's eyes and knew now was the time to stop this big bully from threatening the kingdom ever again. Joey knocked the Ulimate's sword from his hands and tripped him. He held the sword over his face and made him promise to never come near Italy again if Joey let him go. Ultimate hurriedly agreed, and ran off as fast as he could with his hands between his legs.

The battle had ended. Joey had won, and the King pronounced him Joey the Great. The people were very happy. The Ultimate Gildo was gone and so was the illness that had swept the kingdom.

A few years later, the King died. Joey the Great became Joey the Great King, the ruler of the whole Kingdom of Sardinia in Italy. At night, when the moon is shining, sounds of his sword battles can still be heard for miles and miles. However, the fear of the Ultimate Gildo is gone forever.

THE END

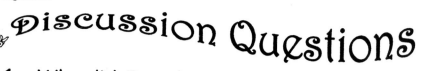

Discussion Questions

1. Who did Joey have to beat to become Joey the Great?
   _____

2. Why did Joey train so much? _____
   _____

3. Why do you think the kingdom was in danger? _____
   _____

4. What do you think would have happened if Joey had lost the fight?_____
   _____

5. Can you retell how Joey won the battle? _____
   _____

6. Do you agree with Joey's promotion to Joey the Great King?
   _____

7. What is the most important point of this story? _____
   _____

True or False

Circle **T**, if the statement is True or circle **F**, if the statement is false.

1. Joey was the King of the Italian Kingdom.   T   F
2. Joey the Great wanted to get rid of the Ultimate Gildo. T   F
3. The story takes place in Africa.   T   F
4. Joey was a knight.   T   F
5. Joey had a wife.   T   F
6. The King gave Joey the title Joey the Great.   T   F
7. When the King died, Joey became Joey the Great King.   T   F
8. People in Italy still fear the Ultimate Gildo.   T   F

An Interview with Joey the Great

Imagine that you could spend an hour with Joey the Great. You are honored about this meeting and you are a little nervous. You want to be prepared. Write five questions you would like to ask Joey the Great.

Q1: _____

Q2: _____

Q3: _____

Q4: _____

Q5: _____

Pretend that you are Joey the Great. Switch papers with a classmate and answer his or her questions.

A1: _____

A2: _____

A3: _____

A4: _____

A5: _____

Prince Artee's Hobby

Prince Artee was a fine prince. He was good and kind. He went to school. The servants who had children found that Prince Artee was a good friend to their children. However, something was missing. Prince Artee wanted a hobby. All the other kids his age seemed to have many interests, hobbies, and fun activities to do but Prince Artee did not. He decided to go to the castle library to look up what kind of hobby he would like.

First, he looked at some music books. That would be fun, he thought. He could learn how to play the harp. But, no, Prince Artee could not get the rhythm. So Prince Artee went to get himself more books.

He got himself some books on building catapults. That would be fun, he thought. He would build a small catapult and throw pumpkins across the kingdom wall. No, Prince Artee was not very good at building things and with his luck, he would be the one struck by a pumpkin. Not a good idea, he thought. So he went to get himself some more books.

These books on acting in a play were just right, he thought. He would join the local drama troop and act. No, Prince Artee could not remember lines and performing in So Prince could not imagine himself front of a huge crowd. Artee went to get himself some more books. Cookbooks made Prince Artee

curious. Cooking would be fun, he thought. He would try all sorts of recipes from scones to roast peacock. No, Prince Artee did not really want to get his hands dirty, and the King wouldn't want him in the castle kitchen. So the Prince went to get himself some more books.

Horses, horses, horses, books about horses. They were many horses in the stables and he could learn how to care for them. No, Prince Artee had a weak stomach and would never clean the stalls. So Prince Artee went to get himself some more books.

Art books. That was another good idea. He could learn how to paint beautiful paintings that would be used to decorate the castle. No, Prince Artee was colorblind and did not like being messy. So Prince Artee went to get himself some more books.

On his way down the castle stairs, he met his younger brother. "Hey Artee, can you show me where   the geography books are? You must know where they   are; you're always in the library."

That is it!
He did not
have to
find
a

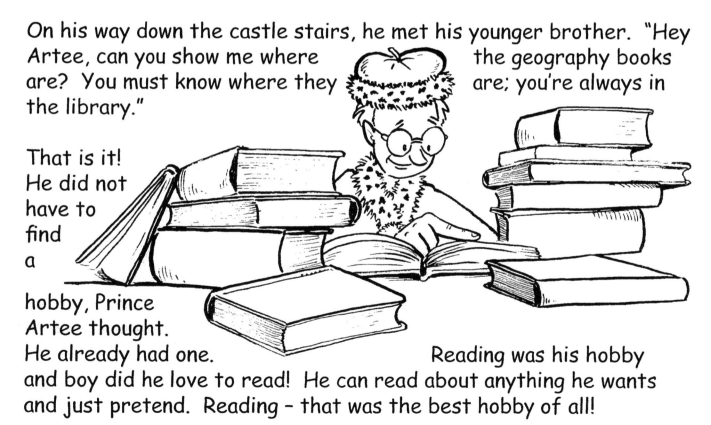

hobby, Prince
Artee thought.
He already had one.   Reading was his hobby
and boy did he love to read! He can read about anything he wants and just pretend. Reading – that was the best hobby of all!

THE END

Discussion Questions

1. What did Prince Artee really want to have? _____

2. Where did Prince Artee decide to go and see if he could find an answer? _____

3. Why was becoming an artist impossible? _____
   _____

4. What would motivate someone to read?_____
   _____

5. Can you think of another possible hobby for Artee and come up with a reason why he could not do it? _____
   _____

6. List the seven hobbies mentioned in the story in the order you would like to do them yourself.

   1. _____   2. _____
   3. _____   4. _____
   5. _____   6. _____
   7. _____

True or False

Circle **T**, if the statement is True or circle **F**, if the statement is false.

1. Prince Artee could not read.   T F

2. There was a library in the castle.   T F

3. Prince Artee was a great cook.   T F

4. Prince Artee could not tolerate the smell of horses.   T F

5. Prince Artee had an older brother.   T F

6. Prince Artee was very lucky.   T F

All You Have to Do Is Name It

Use this ABC Chart to name as many subjects that are interesting to you as you can. For example, A) airplanes B) beaches C) cowboys D) dogs…

A) _____   N) _____
B) _____   O) _____
C) _____   P) _____
D) _____   Q) _____
E) _____   R) _____
F) _____   S) _____
G) _____   T) _____
H) _____   U) _____
I) _____   V) _____
J) _____   W) _____
K) _____   X) _____
L) _____   Y) _____
M) _____   Z) _____

Reading List

Pretend that you will meet Prince Artee next week and he asks you to write a book list for him. Which five books are your favorites? Write the titles and the authors below.

1. _____
2. _____
3. _____
4. _____
5. _____

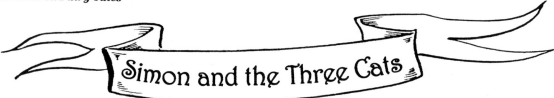

Simon and the Three Cats

Once upon a time in a house in the city lived a two-year-old boy called Simon. Simon had three cats: Fish, Lectra, and Kiwi. Simon followed them everywhere they went.

Each cat had its own bed. Fish had the rocking chair. Lectra had the top of the sofa and Kiwi loved to snuggle on any backpack left on the floor. Simon liked to go and kiss the cats when they were sleeping.

In the washroom, each cat had its own brush. Fish had a hard bristle brush. Lectra had plastic brush for her long fur and Kiwi had a fine-toothed comb. Simon and his Mom took care of their fur everyday.

Neatly laid out on the kitchen floor were three dishes, one for each cat. A large one for Fish, a medium one for Lectra, and a little bowl for Kiwi. Simon would feed them every day.

One day, while Simon's dad was bringing in the groceries, the door was left open and the cats quickly ran outdoors.

When Simon woke up from his nap, Fish, Lectra and Kiwi were nowhere in sight.

"Who's been sleeping in their beds?" thought Simon. He checked the rocking chair, on top of the sofa, and the tote bags on the floor. The cats were not there.

"Who's been wanting their fur brushed?" thought Simon. He checked in the washroom and found the brushes and comb left in their place. The cats were not hiding in the washroom.

"Who's been eating their breakfast?" thought Simon. He went to the kitchen and saw the big bowl, the medium bowl, and the little bowl. They were all empty. The cats were not in the kitchen.

Simon started to cry. He cried for Fish and he cried for Lectra and he cried for Kiwi. His parents searched the entire house and came back empty-handed. They sat in the living room and cried.

Just then, Simon saw Fish, Lectra, and Kiwi outside the living room window. He cried for joy and ran to the window. Simon's dad ran to the door and called the cats.

The cats came in and went to their beds and purred.

Then the cats walked to the washroom where Dad, Mom, and Simon brushed their fur.

After such a nice clean up, the cats went into the kitchen where their bowls were filled once more, and had a snack.

Simon was happy and the cats decided never to run away again.

THE END

Discussion Questions

1. Why did the cats leave the house? _____
_____

2. Where did Simon go when the cats left? _____
_____

3. Why do you think the cats came back? _____
_____

4. Do you think the cats enjoyed being followed everywhere by Simon? _____
_____

5. Can you think of other animals Simon might like?
_____

6. List the belongings of each cat.

Fish	Lectra	Kiwi

True or False

Circle **T**, if the statement is True or circle **F**, if the statement is false.

1. Simon was two years old.   T   F
2. The cats left because they were tired of Simon.   T   F
3. Fish, Lectra, and Kiwi are also food items.   T   F
4. Dad and mom were sad the cats had disappeared.   T   F
5. Hungry cats don't usually go very far.   T   F
6. Simon will continue to follow his cats.   T   F

point-of-View

When writing a story, the author has chosen if she will tell the story or the story will come through one of the characters. Choose either one of the cats, Dad, or Mom and write how they reacted and how they felt when the cats were gone.

_____

_____

_____

_____

_____

_____

_____

_____

Now write how different the story would be if Simon was 6, 16, or 26. Where would the reader see changes?

_____

_____

_____

_____

_____

_____

_____

_____

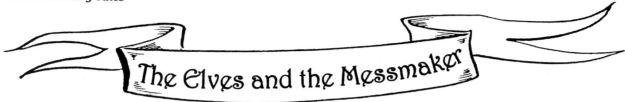

The Elves and the Messmaker

Timmy had become so bad at cleaning his room that the only clean clothes left in his drawers were one pair of socks and an undershirt. There were so many dirty clothes on his floor that it was difficult to tell what color the carpet was!

One night, he picked up the least dirty clothes and placed them on his dresser. This is what I'll wear tomorrow, he thought. He settled in to say his prayers and rapidly fell asleep.

In the morning, he awoke to a beautiful sight. The clothes he had set out the night before had been washed, dried, ironed, and folded and were nicely displayed. Wow, he thought. His mother could not believe her eyes. She was stunned. Timmy was very happy. He quickly got ready and left for school in clean clothes.

That night when Timmy was getting ready for bed, he chose the grimiest pants and the filthiest t-shirt and socks and placed them on his dresser. He said his prayers and promptly fell asleep.

The following morning, the clothes had been washed, dried, ironed, folded, and exhibited in a beautiful fashion.

This went on for many more months. A few nights before Christmas, Timmy asked his mother if she would hide with him in the closet, with the door open just a little bit so they could see what was really happening in his room. His mom agreed. They hid in the closet and left the door ajar.

At midnight, two elves came into Timmy's room. They carried a washbasin, a clothesline, and an electrical iron and board. It took the elves the whole night to clean the clothes, to dry them, to iron them, and to fold them just right. It was a very long and tedious job but the two elves seemed happy to do the work.

Timmy felt terrible. "If I picked up all my clothes and put them in the laundry basket, these elves wouldn't be working so hard at such a tiresome job." Timmy had to find a way to thank the elves.

That day when Timmy came home from school, he collected his dirty clothes and did his laundry. With a little help from his mom, he washed his clothes, dried them, ironed them, folded them and then put them away in his drawers.

Timmy thought the elves were very generous and giving but that he had to take care of his own clothes. Timmy never left any clothes lying around anymore and he always had clean clothes to wear.

That night he set out some cookies with a Thank You note on his dresser. No clothes were in sight. Timmy soon fell fast asleep.

At midnight, the elves came into Timmy's room. They read the note and ate the cookies and were happy they had helped Timmy to grow up. The elves left, never to return again. Instead, they went in search of another messy bedroom... maybe they'll be in yours tonight?

THE END

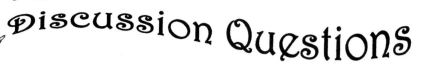

Discussion Questions

1. What did the elves do when they got to Timmy's room?

    _____

2. How did Timmy feel when he realized what the elves were doing?

    _____

3. Why is being clean important?_____

    _____

4. Why didn't Timmy clean his own clothes?_____

    _____

5. Do you think the elves were good to Timmy or not? Explain.

    _____

6. What suggestions could you make to Timmy about cleaning his clothes and his room? _____

    _____

7. What do you think Timmy learned in this story?_____

    _____

True or False

Circle **T**, if the statement is True or circle **F**, if the statement is false.

1. Timmy was a little boy who did not pick up after himself. **T   F**
2. Timmy had a huge family.   **T   F**
3. His mother was upset that she did not have laundry to do. **T   F**
4. The two elves also made shoes.   **T   F**
5. The visits lasted for a few months.   **T   F**
6. Timmy and his mom hid in the closet.   **T   F**
7. Timmy felt terrible when he saw how hard the elves worked. **T   F**
8. Timmy paid them and they stayed until Timmy got married.   **T   F**

synonyms

Synonym means there is more than one word to use to describe an object or feeling. For example, big, huge, and large are synonyms because they are words that mean the same thing. Happy, joyous, excited, and content are also synonyms. In the story "The Elves and the Messmaker", there are many pairs of synonyms. See how many you can find!

new Ending...

Imagine that you are the author of "The Elves and the Messmaker". Go back to the passage where Timmy had to find a way to thank the elves. Rewrite a new ending.

_____

_____

_____

_____

_____

The Right-One Prince

There was once a Princess who wished to marry a Prince, but he had to be a real Prince. She flew all over the world in hopes of finding such a man; but there was always something not right. Princes were readily available but she was finding the wrong ones. She wanted to find the Right-One. She could never find the Right-One. Sad and lonely, she returned home.

One evening during a snowstorm, the Royal Family heard loud banging at the front door. The butler opened the door.

It was a man dressed as a Prince who stood outside the door. Wet with the snow and the sleet, he was in a sad condition. He was shivering and with a stutter he asked the butler if it was true that the Princess was looking for the Right-One Prince. He was convinced that he was that man.

"Ah! we shall soon said not a word quietly into the the bed, and put

see!" thought the Queen-Mother. She of what she was going to do but went bedroom, took all the bed-clothes off 30 little peas on the mattress. She then laid 20 marshmallows between the peas and she also added a few rice cakes. She covered the mattress with the bed sheet and left the guest room.

Upon this bed the Prince was to pass the night.

The next morning the butler asked how he had slept. "Oh, very well indeed!" he replied.

The Queen-Mother was in shock. How could he sleep well with the peas, marshmallows and rice cakes? She ran to the guest room. She pulled the bed sheet off the mattress and saw ...nothing. Nothing was on the mattress. No squashed peas, no squished marshmallows, and no flattened rice cakes. What was she to do?

Every Prince who had claimed to be the Right-One Prince had not slept well and had left a mess on the mattress.

The Queen-Mother went to investigate and asked the Prince, "How well did you sleep"?

"Very well thank you," said the Prince. "Just before I sat on the bed, I took out my pet rat Ralph from my pocket to play with him before bedtime. He sniffed the food under the bed sheet. He ate the peas and I ate the marshmallows and we shared the rice cakes. We were both pleasantly full and fell fast asleep."

The Queen-Mother fainted.

Now it was plain that the man must be the Right-One Prince, since he loved pets and had been wise to have a snack before bed. The Princess was very happy. A wedding for the Royal Couple was planned.

The Princess, the Right-One Prince and the rat Ralph lived happily ever after.

THE END

Discussion Questions

1. Why do you think the Queen-Mother was trying to trick the Prince? _____

    _____

2. Why did she faint? _____

    _____

3. Do you think it a bad idea to have a pet rat? Explain why or why not. _____

    _____

4. What do you think you would have done in the Prince's place?

    _____

5. Compare this story with "The Real Princess" fairy tale. Which ending do you like best? Why? _____

    _____

True or False

Circle **T**, if the statement is True or circle **F**, if the statement is false.

1. The Princess searched all over the world for her Prince. **T   F**

2. She found him during a tornado. **T   F**

3. The Queen-Mother put food under the bed sheet. **T   F**

4. The Prince squashed the food during the night. **T   F**

5. The Prince brought his pet rat named Ralph. **T   F**

6. The pet rat Ralph scared the Royal Family. **T   F**

7. The Royal Family held a Royal Wedding. **T   F**

My Pet Rat

Would you like to have a pet rat? List items you will need before you adopt your pet rat.

_____

_____

_____

_____

Write four names that would be suitable for a pet rat.

1. _____   2. _____

3. _____   4. _____

Noisy Food or Quiet Food

Pretend that you are the Queen-Mother. In the left-hand column, list the noisy food you could put under the bed sheet. In the right-hand column, list quiet foods that would not make noise under the bed sheet.

The Three Little Raccoons

Once upon a time, there were three little raccoons. Their names were Cookie, Cheeks, and Velveteen. They were small, curious, and very fast. They were always looking for food in Mr. and Mrs. Buun's garbage bins.

They visited their garbage bins, getting the lids off, tipping them over, and sniffing through the empty packages. They didn't mean to leave garbage all over the place. It just happened.

Mr. Buun had had enough. He thought if he could find the raccoons' homes and destroy them, they'd have to find another place to live and other garbage bins. The plan was sure to succeed.

On a bright and sunny day, Mr. Buun followed Cookie to the opening of his burrow. It was underneath the shed. Mr. Buun had an idea and went to get the garden hose. He watered under the shed. The water flowed in all directions. Cookie came out and ran with all his might to Cheeks' den, with Mr. Buun following behind.

Cheeks' den was high up in an old hollow tree beside the shed. Both raccoons were very scared as they huddled together up in the tree. Mr. Buun saw where Cookie and Cheeks were hiding and he had an idea. He went to get his chainsaw. He cranked it up and in no time at all, the tree came tumbling down into the yard.

Cookie and Cheeks were scared but unharmed. They ran to their older sister Velveteen's home. She lived in a tree down the street. Mr. Buun thought he would be able to get them now. He followed them into the yard.

He saw a shortcut to the tree by running along the side of the pool. Half way around the pool Mr. Buun started to loose his balance. He swayed a little to the left. He swayed a little to the right. He fell right into the pool.

Oh no, poor Mr. Buun, thought the raccoons. Mr. Buun doesn't know how to swim.

"We can't leave him there," said Cookie.

"We can't get him out of there either," said Cheeks.

"Follow me," said Velveteen, the older sister.

The three raccoons ran with incredible speed right to the garbage bins. They made so much noise that Mrs. Buun came outside to see what was happening. She saw the raccoons but then she also saw Mr. Buun struggling in the water.

Mrs. Buun ran to the pool and threw him a lifebuoy. He finally stopped struggling and hung on tight. She helped him out while the raccoons watched and cheered. Mr. Buun was saved! Everyone was happy!

From that day on, Mr. & Mrs. Buun made sure the raccoons always had plenty of room to play and plenty of food to eat. They never went into the garbage bins again.

THE END

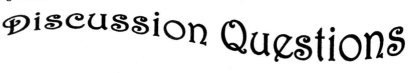

Discussion Questions

1. What did Mr. Buun want to get rid of? _____

   _____

2. Why were Cookie, Cheeks, and Velveteen so terrible? _____

   _____

3. Why was the garbage such a popular place? _____

   _____

4. What could Mr. Buun have done to get rid of the raccoons?

   _____

5. What suggestions would you give Mr. Buun? _____

   _____

6. Which story do you like better, "The Three Raccoons" or "The Three Little Pigs"? Why?

   _____

True or False

Circle **T**, if the statement is True or circle **F**, if the statement is false.

1. Mr. and Mrs. Buun liked garbage on their lawn. **T F**

2. There was a skunk living underneath their balcony. **T F**

3. Cookie lived underneath the shed in the backyard. **T F**

4. Cheeks lived in an old abandoned car. **T F**

5. Mr. Buun was not a good swimmer. **T F**

6. Mrs. Buun came running when she heard noise in the backyard. **T F**

7. Mrs. Buun knew that Mr. Buun was drowning. **T F**

Double Vowels

There are many words in the story "The Three Little Raccoons" that have the double e (**ee**), double o (**oo**) or double u (**uu**). How many can you find?

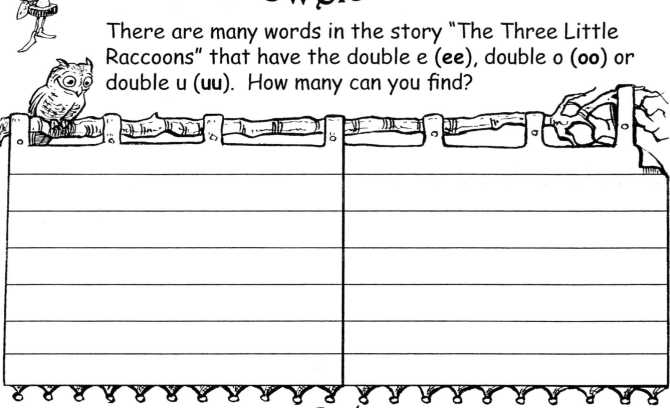

The Written Rules

Imagine that you have just visited Mr. Buun's yard and saw the mess the raccoons made all over the place. The three little raccoons need a list of rules that they must follow to avoid misbehaving at their neighbor's house. Write a list of six rules that raccoons, children, and adults should follow when visiting.

1. _____
2. _____
3. _____
4. _____
5. _____
6. _____

The True Story of Cinderfella

Once upon a time, there was a boy called Cinderfella. Cinderfella lived in a very small house. His mother died and Cinderfella had to stay with his two stepbrothers and his very mean stepfather. Everyone expected Cinderfella to do everything around the house.

Cinderfella had to cut the grass, tend the garden, chop wood for the fire, and get the birds out of the gutters. Many days were spent working while his stepfamily went to fast food restaurants, roller bladed, and played football.

One day while Cinderfella was chopping wood, he saw a strange woman holding a yellow glass vial. She came up to him and said, "I'm your fairy godmother and I'll grant you three wishes".

Cinderfella was annoyed; he had a lot of work to do. "What? I have a fairy godmother? What luck do I have?" He said sarcastically.

"I will grant you three wishes. Go ahead, make one," she insisted.

"All right, I want to go shopping and have so many nice clothes, toys, and books I'll never run out," he said.

OTM-14263 • SSN1-263 Fractured Fairy Tales

"Good choice!" She flicked some liquid from the vial and chanted in a language Cinderfella had never heard before. In no time, new clothes were on Cinderfella and boxes were piled everywhere.

"What's you second wish?" she asked.

"School!" He said, " I want to go to school and get a diploma so I'll be able to get a nice job."

"Good choice!" She flicked some liquid from the vial and chanted in a language Cinderfella had never heard before. In no time, he had schoolbooks and was getting smarter and smarter.

"And now for your third wish," she impatiently asked. She stood waiting as if she had someone else waiting for her.

"Marriage! I want to get married to the Princess. I'll be forced to go and live with her and leave my family behind," he said. He knew that one would be tough, but hey, a wish is a wish.

"Good choice!" She flicked some liquid from the vial and chanted. In no time, the church bells were ringing as Cinderfella and the Princess were married. Together they had many children and lived happily ever after.

25 years later... Cinderfella is still cutting the grass, tending to the garden, chopping wood for the fire, and getting the birds out of the gutter. However, he is also roller blading and playing football. Best of all, he has 10 children to help him with all the chores.

THE END

Discussion Questions

1. What problem did Cinderfella have? _____

   _____

2. What other wishes could Cinderfella have made? _____

   _____

3. Why do you think a stepfather would treat his stepson badly?

   _____

4. How do you feel about making wishes?_____

   _____

5. If you had to ask for three wishes, what would they be?

   _____

6. Who do you think has the best life, Cinderfella or Cinderella?
   Why?_____

   _____

True or False

Circle **T**, if the statement is True or circle **F**, if the statement is false.

1. Cinderfella's mother died.   T   F
2. There were three boys, a father, and two sisters in the family.   T   F
3. Cinderfella was a hard worker.   T   F
4. The godmother was a beautiful fairy.   T   F
5. The godmother granted Cinderfella three wishes.   T   F
6. Cinderfella's wishes were shopping, school, and having children.   T   F
7. 25 years later, Cinderfella had a good life.   T   F
8. The stepfamily came to live with Cinderfella and his wife.   T   F

Double Consonants

There are many words in the story "Cinderfella" that have **double consonants** like (ll), (pp), (tt), (ss). How many can you find?

Agree or Disagree

Cinderfella made three wishes. Think about them. Write below if you think it is a good wish or not. Explain your reasons.

Shopping: _____

_____

_____

Schooling: _____

_____

_____

Marriage: _____

_____

_____

Map the Kingdom

Choose one of the kingdoms from one of the stories. Describe where the kingdom is and in the box below draw the aerial view of the kingdom. Is there a river near by? Mountains?

_____

_____

_____

_____

_____

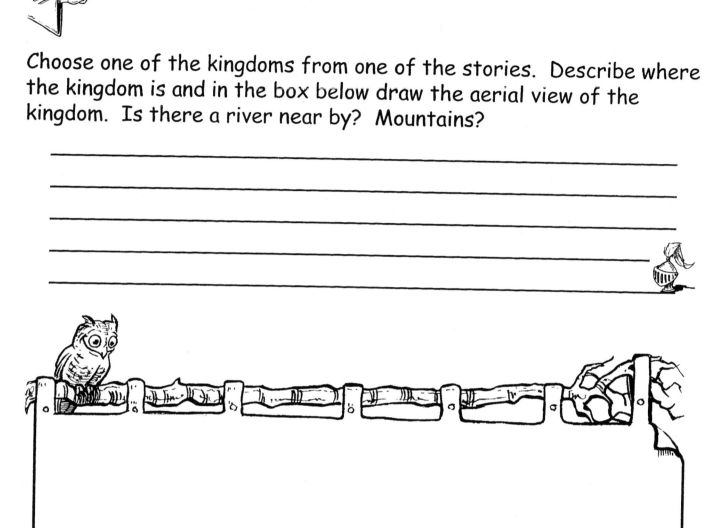

A Party Invitation

Choose one of the characters you would love to invite to one of your parties. Write an invitation card. Do not forget to mention what the occasion is. What refreshments will be served? What music will be heard?

_____

_____

_____

_____

_____

Which Fairy Tale?

Below are some pictures from the fractured fairy tales.
Can you guess what fairy tales these pictures belong to?

1.

_____

2.

_____

3.

_____

4.

_____

5.

_____

6.

_____

7.

_____

8.

_____

your Favorite Sport

What is your favorite sport? Describe the rules and regulations to one of the characters in one of the stories.

_____

_____

_____

_____

_____

A Character Letter

Choose one of your favorite characters from another book you have read. Write to a character from one of the fractured fairy tales. Use the voice of the first character to write the second character a note.

Dear:_____

_____

_____

_____

_____

_____

_____

_____

_____

_____

_____

_____

_____

_____

put Yourself in the Tale

If you could be part of a fairy tale or a fractured fairy tale which one would you choose? Write how you would fit into the story. Draw yourself with the main characters.

_____

_____

_____

_____

Writing Your Own Fractured Fairy Tales

A fractured fairy tale is a story that reminds us of a familiar fairy tale we already know, but with funny changes made to it.

There are many ways you can change a fairy tale. Some changes might be:

- the characters
- the time
- the problem

- the setting
- the point-of-view
- the beginning, middle, or the end

Here are some ways you can make changes:

Change the characters. For example: Change boys to girls, girls to boys, people to animals, animals to people

Change the setting. For example: retell the story in the city versus the country, a shopping mall instead of a castle, or on a beach instead of in the forest.

Change the time the story took place. For example: instead of writing the story in the medieval times, rewrite the story in modern times.

Change the point-of-view. Rewrite the story from one of the minor characters, an opposite character, or from an object such as a fly on the wall, a plant on a table, or a household pet.

Change the problem. Make the problem worse, better or different. You can also change the story from happy to sad or sad to exciting.

Change the beginning, the **middle**, and/or the **end**.

 # Fractured Fairy Tale Story Planner

Familiar fairy tale:_____

New title – fractured fairy tale:_____

Underline two (or more) items you will change in your fractured fairy tale.

- the characters
- the time
- the problem

- the setting
- the point-of-view
- the beginning, middle, or the end

For each change you will make, tell what the familiar fairy tale has and how you will change it in your fractured fairy tale.

Familiar Fairy Tale	Fractured Fairy Tale

Fractured Fairy Tale Story Planner

Title of familiar fairy fale: _____

Title of fractured fairy tale: _____

Draw the character in the familiar fairy tale.

Draw the character in your fractured fairy tale.

Fractured Fairy Tale Story Planner

Title of familiar fairy fale: _____

Title of fractured fairy tale: _____

Tell what happens in the beginning of your fractured fairy tale:

_____

_____

_____

_____

_____

Tell what happens in the middle of your fractured fairy tale:

_____

_____

_____

_____

_____

Tell what happens in the end of your fractured fairy tale:

_____

_____

_____

_____

_____

Fractured Fairy Tale Story Planner

Title of Fairy Tale: _____

New title – fractured fairy tale:_____

Design a book cover for your fractured fairy tale.

Fractured Fairy Tale Story Planner

Title of familiar fairy tale:_____

Title of fractured fairy tale: _____

Write your fractured fairy tale.

_____

_____

_____

_____

_____

_____

_____

_____

_____

_____

_____

_____

_____

Answer Key

Fractured Fairy Tale Word Search: *(page 15)*

```
V E L V E T E E N A
A S M Z S B C L K R
L W O S R M O V I T
L E Z Z Z O E N E
E A Z Z Z K S G E
F T N A I C I G A M
R S H U G E E T S R
E H B L U E I K Z B
D I Z Z Y M E Z Z U
N R Z E M E Z Z Z U
I T O Y H S I M O N
C J A C K N I G H T
```

The Stinky Cheese Man and Other Fairly Stupid Tales: *(page 22)*

Differences:

1. title page is called title page
2. dedication upside down
3. (your name here) for dedication
4. Surgeon General's Warning
5. Intro signed Jack Up the Hill (where's Jill?)
6. falling table of contents on Chicken Licken
7. blank page in the middle of book
8. Giant Story – one sentence from each fairy tale
9. Jack's story-font
10. The tortoise and the hair (hair – hare) and not with gold string is knot
11. cheese in the oven melts
12. skunk can't handle the smell
13. back cover blah blah blah
14. the ugly duck **is** ugly
15. Goldilocks and the Three Elephants, instead of Bears

Collage:

Aesop's picture, magic lamp, golden egg, slipper, evil witch, black cat, gingerbread man, magic wand, snow white's red rose, giant's hand, three different sizes of chairs

Cinderumpelstiltskin: *(page 23)*

1. Cinderella lived…
2. The prince announced…
3. The stepmother and…
4. Cinderella cleaned…
5. "I can help you…"
6. "Would you like…"
7. "Come on. Do you think…"
8. "Oh, just guess a name…"
9. Then she closed the door…
10. They changed her name…

The Stinky Cheese Man: *(page 24)*

Scrambled words:

1. stinky
2. cheese
3. stomachache
4. gagged
5. sneezed
6. teacher
7. bridge
8. coughed
9. awful
10. terrible

The Stinky Cheese Man and Other Fairly Stupid Tales: *(page 25)*

1. Sly Fox
2. The Other Frog Prince
3. The Stinky Cheese Man
4. Really Ugly Duck
5. The Giant
6. Little Red Hen

Friends: *(page 28)*
True or False:
  1. F   **2.** F   **3.** T   **4.** F   **5.** F

Huge Blue Sweatshirt: *(page 32)*
True or False:
  1. T   **2.** F   **3.** T   **4.** F   **5.** T   **6.** F   **7.** T   **8.** F

Adjectives: cute, little, blue, sweat, yummy, golden, red, ripe, warm, fresh, hot, homemade, chicken, huge, delicious, great, big

Test Your Memory:
  1. bird-corn   **2.** raccoon-tomatoes   **3.** wolf-bread and cheese
  4. bear – soup   **5.** blank - there wasn't a cat in the story

Jack and the Beanstalks: *(page 36)*
True or False:
  1. F   **2.** T   **3.** T   **4.** F   **5.** F   **6.** T

Regular verbs: loved, planted, wanted, offered, passed, covered, asked, yelled, showed, delivered, picked, thanked, surrounded

Irregular verbs: was, did, told, had, thought, grew, eat, took, were, make, know, go, run, came, kept, bought, brought, see

Joey the Great: *(page 40)*
True or False:
  1. F   **2.** T   **3.** F   **4.** T   **5.** T   **6.** T   **7.** T **8.** F

Prince Artee's Hobby: *(page 44)*
True or False:
  1. F   **2.** T   **3.** F   **4.** T   **5.** F   **6.** T

Simon and the Three Cats: *(page 48)*
  6. *Fish:* rocking chair, hard bristle brush, and a large bowl
     Lectra: top of sofa, plastic brush, medium bowl
     Kiwi: tote bag, fine-toothed comb, and little bowl

True or False:
  1. T   **2.** F   **3.** F   **4.** T   **5.** T   **6.** T

The Elves and the Messmaker: *(page 52)*
True or False:
  1. T   **2.** F   **3.** F   **4.** F   **5.** T   **6.** T   **7.** T **8.** F

Synonyms: bad-terrible, picked-collected, grimiest-filthiest, placed-set-exhibited-displayed, rapidly-quickly-fast-promptly, open-ajar

The Right-One Prince: *(page 56)*
True or False:
  1. T   **2.** F   **3.** T   **4.** F   **5.** T   **6.** F   **7.** T

The Three Little Raccoons: *(page 60)*

True or False:

  1. T   **2.** F   **3.** T   **4.** F   **5.** T   **6.** F   **7.** F

Double Vowels: three, raccoons, Cookie, Cheeks, Velveteen, looking, food, Buun, succeed, tree, street, pool, poor, loose, speed, see, cheered, room

The True Story of Cinderfella: *(page 64)*

True or False:

  1. T   **2.** F   **3.** T   **4.** F   **5.** T   **6.** F   **7.** T   **8.** F

Double Consonants: called, Cinderfella, small, grass, chopped, gutters, roller, football, tall, will, I'll, yellow, glass, annoyed, shopping, marriage, Princess, sarcastically, married, getting, bells, all

Which Fairy Tale: *(page 68)*

  1. Cinderfella
  2. The Three Little Raccoons
  3. Prince Artee's Hobby
  4. Friends
  5. Jack and the Beanstalks
  6. Huge Blue Sweatshirt
  7. The Elves and the Messmaker
  8. Joey the Great